Ideas for New Businesses

Ideas
for
New Businesses

**Finding ideas for starting your
million or billion-dollar business.**

Wm. Hovey Smith

authorHOUSE®

AuthorHouse™
1663 Liberty Drive
Bloomington, IN 47403
www.authorhouse.com
Phone: 1 (800) 839-8640

© 2015 Wm. Hovey Smith. All rights reserved.

No part of this book may be reproduced, stored in a retrieval system, or transmitted by any means without the written permission of the author.

Published by AuthorHouse 03/20/2015

ISBN: 978-1-5049-0250-2 (sc)

Print information available on the last page.

Any people depicted in stock imagery provided by Thinkstock are models, and such images are being used for illustrative purposes only. Certain stock imagery © Thinkstock.

This book is printed on acid-free paper.

Because of the dynamic nature of the Internet, any web addresses or links contained in this book may have changed since publication and may no longer be valid. The views expressed in this work are solely those of the author and do not necessarily reflect the views of the publisher, and the publisher hereby disclaims any responsibility for them.

Ideas for New Businesses

New Business concepts can easily be grouped as coming from four general areas: introspection, work experiences, life experiences and human interactions. Although three of the four categories involve other people, it is convenient to discuss these categories separately because generating new business ideas is best done by observing situations where new products or services are needed.

Business ideas from introspection

The systematic examination of a person's life with its errors, follies and successes is the basis for all autobiographical writing. This information transfer is the reason that humans have been able to advance at a remarkable pace because each generation did not have to independently derive the previous generations' discoveries. Like an inverted pyramid with a tiny bottom that expands to an enormous top, an initial thought can have exponential expansion when added to by hundreds of generations of human development.

When examining your life, you will find many, "I wish I had done....," kinds of moments. Perhaps you managed a redo on some of these and pointed your life away from threatened disaster towards a more successful direction. When communicated to others, these pivotal life events have led to large numbers of self-help organizations and businesses like Toastmasters, which seek to improve people's communication skills by forcing them to give presentations and overcome their fears of public speaking.

For many this fear of public expression was reinforced by schools that gave grades, and in times past physical punishments, for failures to learn their lessons. This constant pressure to get good grades resulted in some acting as if a heavenly being was keeping score on their every-day activities. This can result in a fear of failure that is so intense that they cannot act on their ideas because someone may have some critical things to say about them. Two truisms are that life is NOT a graded exercise and anything that is worth doing will draw criticism from someone. The more successful your enterprise, the more abundant these criticisms will be – even to the point of threatening to bring legal action against you.

In my own career, I wrote four of the first books about AIDS during a time when there was widespread need for information, but most writers are so fearful of attending conferences where those with AIDS would be present that they dared not write about it. By this time I was an accomplished technical writer and newspaper reporter who had written many professional Geological reports and published a book about the architecture of the homes and plantations of the Thomasville, Georgia, region. I had no medical training, and I was not associated with a research organization.

I did have the world's experts coming to Atlanta for the First International Conference on AIDS to present the most comprehensive information about the disease that had ever been available. Attending this conference, learning the technical terms and being able to summarize various speakers' thoughts enabled me to write the first edition of *Plain Words about Aids*. In the era before electronic publication, I had several thousand copies printed and sold them from my home.

Subsequently, I attended the second international conference in Paris and the third in Washington, D.C., and produced books from those conferences. Although my books filled a need for timely, low-cost, books about a subject that was a "hot" topic, they only sold a few thousand copies and were not commercially successful.

That experience provided some painful lessons about book content, publication and marketing. I improved my writing income by selling two books to conventional publishing houses, self-publishing books as print-on-demand titles, doing E-books and branching out into radio shows and videos. These activities greatly increased my public exposure and resulted in my landing consulting jobs and speaking engagements.

Questions for introspective examination

- What changes in life direction did I take?
- What concepts most influenced my life?
- What purpose did my life accomplish?
- What were my failures?
- What did I learn from my failures?
- What things have I done in my life that would be most helpful to others?

Those who have been fortunate enough to have survived for more than a few decades will have a larger store of life events to draw upon, but even teens or 20-sometings will have at least some material that can be packaged in some way to help others improve their lives.

Business ideas from work

Nearly all improvements in tools came from a craftsman who needed a new tool in order to do a specific process more efficiently. Often, the craftsman made the first prototype himself, worked out the kinks and then produced it commercially. This first product might even be the anchor product that was followed by more of the craftsman's related inventions that ultimately grew into a company with hundreds of employees. Not only might a new tool be produced, but perhaps even a new manufacturing method.

Henry Ford's assembly lines were the marvels of their age. These assembly lines allowed complete automobiles to roll out of the factory every few minutes instead of taking a month to build a car. Nothing is created in a vacuum. A century before, Ely Whitney made guns with interchangeable parts produced on dedicated assembly lines that allowed national arsenals and private manufacturers to make millions of identical guns during the American Civil War.

With assembly-line production, each new rifle required a unique set of machines that would have to be designed and more factory space added to house the machinery to make each new gun. Modern Computer Numerical Controlled (CNC) machines radically changed this concept because the same equipment can be programed to make differently-shaped parts by loading a new program. The same factory space that once made one model of gun can now be used to make a dozen models, any of which can be quickly returned to production as dictated by consumer demand.

While it is still not possible to throw a pint of whisky into the maw of Robbie The Robot and have him run off 1,000 copies, as was seen in the 1956 movie Forbidden Planet, a CNC equipped factory can machine an unlimited number of related products from the same equipment without having to expand the factory or hire new employees. Similarly, the newer concept of 3-D printing of parts adapted from World War II-era metal stamping techniques can make complex objects by fusing different layers of materials onto a previously printed substrate.

Any inventor who can stay modestly informed about new manufacturing methods, or can hire someone who keeps abreast of new technologies, will discover that techniques like investment casting, sintering or even nanotechnology might enable his new product to be made less expensively by contracting parts out to specialty companies. Boeing, the aircraft company, adapted this technique from the automotive industry to the extent that its aircraft parts are received from dozens of producers to be assembled in huge plants in Seattle and elsewhere.

With just-in-time delivery, inventory costs are reduced, less warehousing space is needed and fewer people are needed to stock items. Automated production has increased to the point that large production facilities run their night shifts with only a handful of highly skilled employees who are often outnumbered by the staff of the companies' contracted security services.

Knowledge-based companies assisted by fast computers, cloud storage and capable computer programs can regularly interact with tens of thousands of subscribers, generate vast amounts of correspondence and how-to videos using only two or three people to manage a multi-million-dollar business. The internet is crowded with experts who will, with varying degrees of competence, assist with list building, database management, semi-automatic communications, content publication, distribution and money management. A successful knowledge-based company can consist of one creative guy, a computer-based-business marketing expert and an accountant. Most services can be contracted out, such as inventory control and shipping.

Ideas are built by combining and restructuring established business models and previously-developed techniques in new ways to make your business concept profitable as quickly as possible. The faster your concept can be converted into reality with the fewest people, the more attractive your new company will be to investors and the more profitable it will be for you.

Derive business ideas from work

Business ideas can be inspired by every-day work activities by taking the following steps:

- Listing your tasks
- Learn how coworkers accomplish theirs
- What new inventions or methods will make the production process more efficient?
- Construct prototype or draft a new operational plan
- Test your concept
- Refine your concept
- Put into full scale operation
- Evaluate and adopt a process of continual improvement

There is a strong possibility in some hind-bound companies that your thoughts will be considered "out of your pay grade," and they will be instantly rejected. This was not because your idea had no merit, but because you originated them. If this is the case and you are confident of your concept, either go to another branch of the same company or change companies so you can work for employers who are more accepting of your inventive nature. If these two options do not appear practical at the moment, form your own company while still working for your present employer and continue to refine your idea.

Some employment contracts are so binding that you must obtain a release to independently develop your new idea or take on an independent project. Even then, there may be a non-competition clause that can prevent you from making products in the same field or working for a competitor or related business for a year or more after you leave the business.

Violation of these contractual obligations can result in expensive, time-consuming litigation that a corporation can afford, but an individual cannot. In short, you may be screwed unless you are committed to be a career man for life, or until your company decides that your services are no longer required.

Even if you started out working for a good company and were given assurances by the owner that such a thing would never happen, these assurances are worthless if the company is bought out and a new management team comes in to make a "leaner and meaner" company. The new owner's goal may be to squeeze maximum short-term profits to increase the company's stock price before flipping it.

Union shops are the most stifling environment for producing new ideas. With strict separation of job categories and work rules that do not allow cross-training between different fields, a worker may become very good at a particular job, but be prevented from contributing to other fields. There is nothing in human history that requires that a person be stuck doing one job or be in one profession all of his life. Yet, this is exactly how the union model works. If you are a machinist, you can think about building traditional machines or even CNC designs, but you may not change a light bulb in your office. This sort of thinking is as Medieval as the guild system from which it originated. Such thinking has no place in a creative organization where cross-fertilization between different professions and fields of knowledge is often the path to new inventions.

There was considerable argument in the early part of the 20th century if it was advantageous to convert mills from water power and belt drives to electricity. Doing away with thousands of feet of slapping belts working pulleys and gears and replacing them with electric motors saved money, reduced the size of the work force, provided a dependable source of power and reduced the size of the manufacturing plant. Electricity also removed the need for industrial plants to be located on rivers with sufficient gradients to operate waterwheels and turbines.

None of the innovations that make modern society could, or would, have come without some individual having the courage to originate new manufacturing concepts and adapt them to existing operations or build new plants incorporating the latest technology closer to the sources of raw materials or markets.

Life experiences

Report your life

Many people are amazed to learn that what they do is of any interest to anyone else, and in fact that people will pay money to learn the skills that they have. They take the position that, "If I can do it, then everyone else must be able to do it as well or better than me."

I don't care what it is. There is someone who needs to be taught how to sweep and clean floors. The same can be said about dish washing, bathroom cleaning, setting tables, making beds, etc. All these life skills must be learned and someone must teach them. In this disjointed society, these tasks are often no longer taught by parents and grandparents either because they are working multiple jobs and do not have time, or energy, to impart these basic life skills to their kids.

When these kids who have had their lives filed with school, social activities and on-screen time are on their own, they find that they need to learn how to keep house, wash clothes, cook and what are somewhat quaintly called, "tasks of everyday living." There first stop for information is often a YouTube video.

Another need for this basic life skill information is for those who have suffered traumatic brain injuries in combat or who have had strokes and must relearn these basic tasks. They do not want to watch children's programs to pick up this information, but want to have it presented by an adult.

Even if you have had a complicated and troubled life caused by by-polar disorders with drug and/or alcohol addiction, and have lived with these problems, you have something to say to others who are still struggling. Everyone has their own mental and physical challenges, and some are willing to pay serious money for others to help them through their difficulties. At the least, your life has been interesting and can serve as a life lesson to others through expression as comedy, blogs, books, radio, TV shows or other means.

If you have something significant to say based on your life experiences, there are those who only you can reach that you can help. There is a place for many sincere and caring voices, even if they are delivering a similar message. Not only is helping others personally fulfilling, it can also be profitable. If you really want to help others and learn to do it well, the money will follow.

Many famous figures from sports, the movies and industry have founded non-profit organizations to promote causes that they are interested in. Often the spur that prompted this action was some event in their lives that forcefully brought a human need to their attention that they felt compelled to answer.

Break-through concepts

There is a degree of truth in the statement, "There are no original ideas, only repackagings of old ones." However, this is not altogether true, and I make it a point of honor that my books, inventions and consulting efforts are original, while acknowledging past influences. There are, and will be, novel ideas. Perhaps song writers have the greatest problems producing completely new materials, since rips of other's songs and lyrics are continuously circulating in their brains and may be unconsciously incorporated into their own material.

Novelists have the difficulty that seemingly every aspect of human relations that could be exposed in a novel has been already written about, and it is difficult to craft a character that is not similar to someone else's hero. Fiction writers must mix this combination of commonly appreciated plot lines that readers like with sufficient new locations, characters and action sequences to make a book that the public will buy. Science fiction writers who constantly probe the new and unknown consistently come up with more provocative ideas than those writing other kinds of books. If a would-be inventor is thinking about how to find undiscovered new trends, reading science fiction is a reasonable tool to use.

Where do new ideas come from, and how do you evoke original thoughts? Since the 1960s, and actually long before, drugs were thought to be the pathway to creativity when the mind went on some wild trips. Even groups like the Beetles produced some drug-inspired materials, but the results, while creative, often had devastating impacts on the performers. Being stoned during business meetings is not likely to elicit a favorable response from investors, no more than a drunken poet is likely to sell his books to acquisition librarians.

Building from an existing knowledge base is the predominate way that new business are propagated, but new-concept creation usually comes from an idea that is so radically different that your first thought might be, "This can't possibly work." But it can. Although new, the product might not be widely embraced, like paper made from processed elephant dung. These large mammals do the mechanical grinding of the wood and do a good job of liberating the non-digestible cellulose fibers that can be made into writing papers. This is an interesting wrinkle in paper-making technology that might have appeal to elephant lovers and have some novelty aspects, but elephant-dung paper is not likely to be the foundation product for a new multi-billion-dollar corporation.

Although I am not an expert on elephant dung, the rounded droppings from moose that litter the Alaskan landscape could be used the same way to make some interesting note cards, provided sufficient quantities of the raw material could be collected. If you have nothing else to do in your cabin during a long Alaskan winter, there is a modest demand for hand-made papers.

A useful commercial concept came to me while I was writing this section. This is "Hand Dancing." Everyone has at some times drummed his fingers to a piece of music, and playing air-guitar has evolved into something of an art form. However, Hand Dancing, where all that is shown are a person or people's hands responding to a piece of music, is unknown in modern society, except perhaps as a technique used in physical therapy. Hands are among a person's most distinctive features, and a video of different pairs of hands responding to a piece of music would be an interesting way to provide live input to a music video, without the costs of making a film that might run $5,000 a minute.

I can envision a small market for hand dancing videos in physical rehabilitation where hands responding to different speeds of music could encourage finger and wrists movements to help exercise tendons, muscles and help keep joints free. A brief period of hand dancing would also be useful for writers and programmers who spend long periods of keyboard time to help prevent carpal tunnel syndrome. Is anyone marketing such a concept at present? Not that I know of, or at least not on a national scale. Could someone take Hand Dancing and make a profitable home business with a website, blogs and videos about it and build a significant worldwide market? Certainly they could. Taken to full development, this could even be a new music category in popular culture with different song writers using Hand Dancing to provide animated expression to their music.

Human interactions

Capturing ideas from others

Who are these "others?" The other person that may be the most significant factor in your discovery of a new business concept might be your spouse, child, friend or a stranger whose conversation you overheard. Anyone in any situation might originate an idea that germinates in your mind and ultimately grows into a new business. Everyone in the world can be your research staff, if you pay attention to what is going on around you.

Some may have even tried their new business and failed. Can you take the same factory or concept and do a turn-around? If that is not possible, can you conceive of a better manufacturing method or location to produce that product at a profit? Was it poor marketing that doomed the product to obscurity? Was it well intentioned, but bad management, that caused the company to fail? Billion-dollar corporations have been built by turn-around specialist who successfully restructured business that had excellent brands, but did not adopt more efficient manufacturing or marketing efforts before it was too late to save the company.

A common appeal from owners of failing businesses is for new capital to meet payrolls and pay bills. Putting new capital into a failing business may work if the new companies' owners did not realize the full costs of their start-up efforts, but the business concept is sound and the management is capable of running the company. Under this limited circumstance, additional investments might provide an inexpensive buy-in for a promising business. More commonly, pouring additional money into a failing company that refuses to make structural changes will only temporarily postpone the company's failure.

Recording your ideas

Most people have a lap top that is two or three generations old that still works which may be an ideal instrument to record your ideas, rank them and examine the concepts in more detail. When working on new ideas, I often use a computer where I have on-line access along with my old Vista laptop. These are on adjacent desks, and all I need to do is to turn in my chair to work on one or the other of the computers. I do mental examinations of my business concepts on my Vista and, when appropriate, transfer the files to thumb drives if I need to send them to someone else. This way I have my work on my own computer that is never put on line and it is safe from hackers or prying corporate eyes.

Once you have progressed to the point where you must share information, exchanging thumb drives between collaborators is a surer way to keep your business concept private than any "secure server" or cloud-storage method. This method also necessitates that you have back-ups in the way of paper documents or on other storage media, because all mechanical devices will ultimately fail.

Everyone works differently. Because I am a writer, I find that it is appropriate for me to take a concept and examine it by outlining it and perhaps writing a few paragraphs. This is a better capture of my thoughts than attempting to remember, "What was that all about?" The writing process enables me to better rank these concepts in the order of when and how I should develop them.

Recording ideas can be done by using some or all of the following methods:

- Keep a notebook
- Take an old laptop and make this your idea computer

- Start a private cloud-based file that you can access from anywhere on any computer
- Recorded video/message on Smart Phone
- Send yourself a text message
- Call your home phone and leave a message of an idea

A computer file with hundreds of ideas has no value unless they are acted upon. As a writer, I exorcise my ideas, which I consider intellectual demons, by producing creative content, but first I must decide which have the best chances of success in which media. My basic decisions are reduced to consideration of in what order and in what manner will I approach them. Will these be books, E-books, blog posts, radio shows or videos? A similar business-related ranking might be, "Is this appropriate for me as a business that I operate myself, do I need partners or is this something to package and sell to a corporation?" These questions will be considered in follow-up books.

Although there are security issues with cloud storage, there is no better existing media to allow real-time relatively secure interchange through encrypted files. When the time comes that partners need to be brought in or collaborators sought to contribute their expertise, being able to store and access data from any place in the world has enormous advantages. It is not unusual for me, for example, to be working with collaborators in Europe or Asia.

There is a time for sharing and collaborating in the business development process, but there is an equal need for private time and space to record, develop and consider your ideas on a regular basis. Perhaps the first Thursday of the month should be your Concept Evaluation Day, which makes more sense than pants-less

Thursdays, or whatever the latest outrageous marketing plan might be from a maker of men's underwear who is seeking national attention. Once a month may be an appropriate time interval for you to explore your new business concepts. This private time might also be while you are on flights to Europe, Asia or Australia. Whenever, select a time where you dedicate to the careful examination of new business concepts. You can even take a mini-vacation and stay in a hotel at say, Nags Head, North Carolina, in mid-Winter to work on your ideas. At Nags Head you will have all the amenities that you need, empty beaches in one of the most scenic areas of North America and be as alone as you wish to be with your thoughts and ideas.

Exposing yourself to creative situations

The fear of change is so strong in some people that they need to receive constant positive reinforcements that change is O.K. and can be successfully accomplished. Doing a variety of things to be exposed to creative situations is always helpful. Attending creative gatherings in or outside of your field, presenting papers and talking to others will help to stir your mental juices and provoke action on your part. One never knows what potentially useful contact might be made or how any given conference will result in some positive financial result. Among the things you might do are:

- Attend meetings and conferences outside of your field
- Regularly interchange with non-profit organizations
- Belong to professional organizations

- Use tools like LinkedIn to learn about the activities of others
- Review business magazines
- Look for concepts that push the edges of existing technology

You do not have to be around large groups of people to maintain a high level of creative thought, but it is helpful to be removed from your comfort zone and listen to what people in non-related fields have to say. Ted Talks are amazing events where a variety of speakers from various fields are brought together to present some ground-breaking concepts about their fields of expertise. Often, these serious talks are broken by comedians who provide their own contributions to the creative arts in an entertaining way. Even if you do not derive any ideas directly from the speakers, you will certainly be inspired.

Not all knowledge, even if it is on a serious topic, must be presented in an academic fashion. As I am working on this book I am also producing non-related videos, including one which is a humorous, but informative video on sexually transmitted diseases. This YouTube video presents itself as a video-recorded visit to Bob, who is a 16 year-old whose family had sent him to a local clinic for testing because they feared that he had been sexually active. This subject material has a lot of comedic potential that even includes slicing up a sausage and sending the young man to the bathroom to demonstrate his mastery of the subject material with a follow-up discussion of the result. You can view this video at: http://youtu.be/34_3F-Tu_BE.

Next Steps

Once you have conceived of a number of business concepts the challenges are to select which among them has the best chance of success and how and when to develop them. I have several things to help you make this decision. Among these are a series of 20 YouTube videos on the Hovey Smith Channel which takes the business process of starting your own outdoor-based business from conception to arranging for its disposal when you die. These may be viewed anytime and are free. The first of the series may be seen at: http://youtu.be/aA7J2folUyU.

This E-book is based on part of a chapter in my forthcoming book *Profit* which will be published in 2015. This video may be seen at: http://youtu.be/DUQJU56vxjU.

Also on my website www.hoveysmith.com, you can sign-up for one one-hour telephone consultation at a deeply discounted rate of $200 an hour by sending an E-mail to hoveysmith@bellsouth.net that describes what you want to discuss. If I feel that I can help you with this issue, we will arrange for a teleconference with you and your associates. After the conference you will receive a written report with my recommendations. Although payment must be given in advance, you can obtain a full refund if you feel that you did not receive adequate value for your money.

If you would like to have something in a fun audio format I have a Podcast Radio Show, "The backyard business conclave at the Road Kill Café," which may be heard on WebTalkRadio.net. Just access the episode at: http://webtalkradio.net/Shows/HoveysOutdoorAdventures/053011.mp3.

My objective in all of these efforts is to provide you with solid information about how to select what business is most appropriate for you and give you a sometimes fun and sometimes provocative kick in the butt to get you started. The opportunities for starting a million or even billion-dollar business are in your head. These ideas only need to be recovered, recognized, evaluated and put into action.

Start recording your ideas in the following Idea Log and notebook. Get busy before someone else beats you to your concept.

To order additional copies and for information on other Profit series book, go to my website: www.hoveysmith.com

Short-Term Ideas

Date	Concept	Action

Short-Term Ideas

Notes

Short-Term Ideas

Notes

Short-Term Ideas

Notes

Short-Term Ideas

Notes

_____

_____

_____

_____

_____

_____

_____

_____

_____

_____

_____

Short-Term Ideas

Notes

Short-Term Ideas

Notes

Short-Term Ideas

Notes

Medium-Term Ideas

Date	Concept	Action

Medium-Term Ideas

Notes

Medium-Term Ideas

Notes

Medium-Term Ideas

Notes

Medium-Term Ideas

Notes

Medium-Term Ideas

Notes

Long-Term Ideas

Date	Concept	Action

Long-Term Ideas

Notes

Long-Term Ideas

Notes

Long-Term Ideas

Notes

Long-Term Ideas

Notes

Long-Term Ideas

Notes

Long-Term Ideas

Notes

www.ingramcontent.com/pod-product-compliance
Lightning Source LLC
Chambersburg PA
CBHW070715180526
45167CB00004B/1481